# DISCIPLES OF

# THE EMPTY TOMB

## Brandon Renfroe

### FOREWORD BY CHUCK WEBSTER

# DISCIPLES OF THE EMPTY TOMB

To my wife, Amanda,
for loving me—
and to "the kids"
Breanna, Leah, Hadley, and Jackson


"Because, if you confess with your mouth that Jesus is
Lord and believe in your heart that God raised him from
the dead, you will be saved."
(Romans 10:9)

"When the sun shines on the yellow leaves,
I think the trees are so pretty.
And the sun was shining today."
Eleanor Renfroe,
My Mother

"He can be as real to you as anybody.
He *can* be, he *must* be, because he's risen."
Timothy Keller

# Table of Contents


Foreword
by Chuck Webster — 1

Introduction
"Disciples of the Empty Tomb" — 5

Chapter 1
"The Importance of the Resurrection" — 19

Chapter 2
"Defending the Resurrection" — 35

Chapter 3
"Living Out the Resurrection" — 55

Chapter 4
"A Better Resurrection" — 73

Recommended Reading on the Resurrection — 85

Afterword
by Drew Kizer — 89

# Foreword
# Chuck Webster

Mark Twain once wrote, "I can live for two months on a good compliment."

I remember when I met Brandon. I was preaching a series of sermons at the church he was serving, and after I finished, he came over and encouraged me.

When you've been preaching for long at all, you learn to distinguish between run-of-the-mill, I've-got-to-say-something-nice compliments and the other kind—the genuine, I-really-mean-this remarks. One is required by the occasion and is appreciated; the other comes from the heart and is cherished . . . and remembered.

Brandon's comments were of the second variety, and not because what he heard was delivered with any above-average ability. He loved Jesus, and he loved hearing people talk about Jesus. The words he shared with me that day—and everything I've heard from him since—come from someone who's genuinely seeking to follow Jesus and who's living his life so that he blesses everyone he meets.

That interaction was much longer than two months ago, but for me Twain's remarks have proved prescient. Brandon's encouragement—which, I suspect, he has long since forgotten—still lifts my spirits all these years later.

That's one of the reasons you should read this book. Brandon loves you, and he wants what's best for you. He's not writing to make money, get famous, or put his church on the front of *Christianity Today*.

He's writing because he wants you to believe that the tomb they put Jesus in on Friday was empty on Sunday morning, because that makes all the difference.

Seriously. There's no hidden agenda.

He's writing because he knows what will happen to you when you believe it, and not just in a probably-so, maybe-so kind of way.

He knows if you peek your head inside the tomb like Mary did—and you see what she saw—Jesus will grab your heart.

That's what happened to Brandon, and that's why he's writing this to you.

But there's another reason to read.

I know this seems silly, but I wish I could go back to school and sit in one of Brandon's science classes. If I could, I'm almost certain that I'd enjoy science more than I did the first time around. Even more importantly, I bet I'd learn more science—how it works, why it matters, why I needed to know it—because Brandon would make the learning experience itself enjoyable.

Here's why that matters: As you'll learn soon enough, Brandon is an excellent teacher. At his core that's who he is. Not the kind of teacher who's just trying to get to the 3:15 go-home bell, but the kind who loves what he's doing and who makes you look forward to class because you know you'll learn something cool. Not just facts and tables and lists that you forget soon after the final exam. In his class you learn why things matter, and you find yourself getting excited because *he's* excited.

As enthusiastic as I suspect Brandon gets about the periodic table—and as much as he knows about how science works—he's even more delighted about what he shares in this book.

He's genuine, he's clear, he's passionate, and he's honest.

He writes simply enough to engage the theological newcomer, but deeply enough to enlighten the advanced.

When you read this book, you'll find yourself getting to know Brandon, because his personality leaps off the pages. He'll make you laugh, and he'll fill you with wonder. He'll challenge you, and he'll bless you.

When you finish reading, you'll walk away from it with a deeper appreciation for Jesus. You'll happily anticipate that coming day when the Lord's resurrection becomes yours.

So grab a cup of coffee and sit down with Brandon. Listen to the heart of a teacher who loves you.


Chuck Webster, Minister
Hoover (AL) Church of Christ
April 2020

# Introduction
# Disciples of the Empty Tomb

**Together One Last Time**

My sweet wife, Amanda, turned 24 on May 3, 2003. (Don't do the math here—it's considered very impolite.[1]) We celebrated her birthday with dinner—and the requisite chocolate cake[2]—at her parents' house in Rainsville, Alabama.

I remember a few things from that day. I recall, for example, eating potato salad on the back porch with Amanda's "Mamaw" (her dad's mother, not to be confused with "Granny," her mom's mom).

I was especially close with Mamaw. Once, back when Amanda and I were dating, Mamaw sent me a birthday card with $10 in it. She wrote inside the card: *"Use this money to take Amanda to McDonald's. If she's good, let her play in the play area."*

Oh my. How could you not *instantly* love someone like that?

But I mainly remember my dad. He was recovering from a couple of surgeries on his leg. His left femoral artery kept clotting, and the doctors were having a tough time fixing it. They tried an artificial artery, then a cadaver one. But

---

[1] She's 40, as of this writing. But you didn't hear that from me.

[2] If you live in or near Fyffe, Alabama, these cakes are made by a lady named Carolyn. You'll need to do the rest of legwork on that…but you'll thank me.

nothing worked. Finally, in January 2003, it seemed they were able to correct the problem.

"You're looking good," I said, as he walked into the house that day. I remember giving him a piece of candy—a peanut butter log. (This is a candy that, generally-speaking, is relished only by the elderly. If you are even aware of it, and are under 40, consider yourself an old soul.)

At some point dad motioned to me, "Let's go outside." He wanted to walk around Amanda's parents' house. It was the first time he'd seen it. Admittedly, it's a big house. Bigger than any my dad ever lived in, for sure. Born in 1933, he had grown up farming, then joined the U.S. Navy in the early 1950s, before retiring in 1971. He then went to work for the government, working on the scopes for the M1A1 Abrams tank. He called the little house we lived in a "cracker box"—a description that still makes me laugh.

When we were out of earshot, he asked me: "How much do you think this place cost?" Almost as if the question were indecent.

"I don't know," I said. "I bet it was a bunch."

At some point during this outdoor excursion, he wanted to look at my mother-in-law's rose bushes that she carefully tended. What happened next is imprinted in my mind.

As I watched him admire the roses, I consciously took a few steps back, viewing my dad almost in panoramic mode. I'm not sure why I did it, but I guess it was understandable. He had been sick, and now was doing better. He was savoring the roses he loved to grow back home. And I was savoring getting to see him healthy again.

I said a prayer for him, if only in my heart. That God would take care of him. That everything would be okay. Tears began to fill my eyes—and that's when you know you had better do something quickly, or you're going to be in trouble. I composed myself, but not before I saw dad give me a curious glance—as if to say, "What in the world are you doing?" It was subtle, but I remember it. It registered with me. He had caught me.

Before he and mom left for the return trip, I told him I would see him again soon. The grass needed cutting on the "Goat Farm"—our family plot of land, a few miles from their house in Piedmont—and I promised I'd come up in a few days to mow it. "Okay," he said. I told him something else, but I can't remember it just now. I know that he nodded. Then they left for home.

Later that night, he died in his sleep.

He was 69 years old.

The next morning the phone rang with the awful news from my sister: "Daddy has died." I don't remember a whole lot after that…but I do remember lying down on the floor.

Daddy was gone.

Like Joseph, I had been the child of my parents' old age. Dad was only a month shy of 45 when I was born. Mom had just turned 40. (I have an older brother, who was born in 1963. My sister, who has since passed away, was born in 1958. And then I came along, in 1978.) Now, with a seven-year-old son of my own, I sometimes think to myself: "At this point in my dad's life, I was not even born." I don't know if that makes me feel young, exactly, but it does put things in a certain perspective.

With my sister getting married when I was only three, and my brother leaving home when I was still in elementary school, for all intents and purposes I was an only child.[3] That is, for parts of three decades…from at least 1987 until 2001, when I got married…it was just me, mom, and dad. I tried to be a good son. On some days, I think I might have been.

You would have to understand my parents, especially my mother, I think, to understand me. And that's really **not** what this book is about—I'm reminding myself of that as I type, I promise—but there are still a few things you need to know, if you're going to appreciate what I want you to appreciate.

My parents didn't get out much. Not after November of 1978, at least.

Before I was born, due to my dad's being in the Navy, my parents had lived in Virginia, Rhode Island, and Illinois. But after my birth, Piedmont was the epicenter of their lives.[4] I think the general feeling was, they had already raised two kids, and so, when I came along in their later years, they deserved credit for time served. And it's not

---

[3] I'm not sure why (then again, maybe I am), but when I was in 10th grade, a girl asked me: "Are you an only child?" "No," I said. But my science teacher, Mrs. Wilson, said, "He basically is." Bless my heart.

[4] From the road sign in town during my childhood: "Welcome to Piedmont, Little Town of Big Opportunities."

like I had a bad childhood. I didn't. This isn't that kind of book. I mean, we went to Disney World in 1985, for crying out loud.[5]

It was just…interesting. Folks often mistook my parents for my grandparents. My best friend in eighth grade, Kevin Lockridge, even asked me, "Brandon, how does it feel to have older parents?"

Let's see. My parents' favorite restaurant was Captain D's. We'd go there on special occasions, like my mom's birthday. When it came my turn to order, the girl at the cash register would ask a youthful me, "What would you like to drink?" And I'd say, "Coke" or "Dr. Pepper" or whatever fizzy drink the good folks at Captain D's had on tap. Then my mother would turn and immediately, invariably say to me: "But we have those at home! Don't you want something else?" I'm not sure what she wanted me to order instead. Maybe something exotic, like sweet tea.

In later years, when I would recount these stories to my parents, reliving the "Wonder Years," they would cast a suspicious glance my way. Mom would always ask, "Is that going to be in the book you're writing about us one day?"

"Probably not," I would say.

*Probably* not.

---

[5] Though I will say this. My mother thought she had lost me on our Disney trip, when I was 6. She went on a frantic search to look for me. I was safely back on the Disney train, with the rest of my family, waiting on mom when she returned, empty-handed…I always thought a little too quickly.

I could tell you other stories, believe me.[6] But I fear you're losing patience with me as it is, so I had better move the narrative along.

I preached the morning my dad died, if you can believe it. It was a Sunday. And since I was a twenty-four-year-old preaching student, I felt I had no choice but to fulfill my duties to the congregation that agreed to have me, in Morris, Alabama. I don't remember much about the sermon, to be honest. I do remember one kindly brother standing before the congregation afterwards and saying to me, "I don't know how you did it, friend."

It's funny the things you remember.

In the South, as in most places, funeral customs vary from state to state, and even within cities. Where I grew up, a couple of days after someone died, you typically had a "visitation," during which people would come to pay their respects to the grieving family. These would typically be in the evening, with the funeral to follow the next day.

Just before the funeral service, there is usually a "last viewing." These are especially emotional moments, sacred moments, when the family says their last goodbyes before the coffin finally is closed. When it came time for my dad's last viewing, my mother reached for my hand and said, "Let's you, me, and him go be together one last time."

A few weeks later, I went to see my mom. While there, I thumbed through an old *Sports Illustrated*. In his weekly

---

[6] Like the time I was learning to ride a bicycle and crashed into our concrete birdbath, rending the top from the bottom. Mother ran from the front porch as I lay on the ground, maimed. "You broke my birdbath!" she said. I was okay.

column, Steve Rushin excerpted Joe Queenan's new book, *True Believers*. One paragraph stood out to me.

> Human life is filled with experiences that seem quite ordinary at the time and assume a fabled stature only with the passage of the years. The little boy out for the day with his father does not know that he will one day be an old man who can walk into a room and dispense the jaw-dropping news that he once saw Babe Ruth and Ty Cobb in the flesh, and deliver it with the same matter-of-factness as saying, "I was with Lee at Antietam."

At the time, of course, I could only think about the day I had just spent with my dad. His last full day on earth.

A day that would change my life, though I hardly realized it at the time.

## We Are Disciples of the Empty Tomb

I guess this is the point where I say, "I said all that to say this."

Nearly two decades have passed since my dad died in 2003. Though I certainly haven't forgotten him, life has steadily moved on. I have four children he never met, my oldest daughter being born three years after his death.

Since August of 2003, I have preached at least part-time. From 2014-2018, I served as an associate minister at a congregation in Calhoun County, Alabama. One Sunday in August 2014, we had a guest speaker.

His name was Terry Edwards.

Many of the regular church members were gone that day, attending a popular religious conference. Even the sound booth guys were absent, which was especially unfortunate, as the speaker's topic that day was "Archaeology and the Bible."

As anyone with walking-around sense knows, a preacher discoursing on an archaeological theme is going to make use of visual aids. In this case, the ubiquitous PowerPoint. Only it wasn't working that day.

Of course it wasn't.

So, for the forty-five minutes that was Mr. Edwards' Bible class, the audience was treated to a cornucopia of flashing images: a green screen initially, quickly followed by a shot of the church parking lot, followed in turn by miscellaneous security camera footage, looped over and over again. It was very existential. I later learned that it garnered several Academy Awards.

Finally, reason won out, and the decision was made to ditch technology for the morning sermon. I felt sorry for the brother, truly I did, but there was no other way.

To be honest, I don't recall much that he said that day. Not that it wasn't a good lesson…it was just six years ago.

But I remember one thing.

I remember it, because it changed my life.

That sounds melodramatic, doesn't it? But I believe it's accurate.

During the climax of his lesson, Edwards said this:

*"We are all disciples of the empty tomb."*

Even if my mind needed several years to process the full import of his thesis, my heart took note of it immediately. The seed was planted. It just needed time to blossom. And when it finally did, it opened new vistas.

Rather than bombard you with flowery phrases—literally—that tend to annoy me, let me try to explain in more concrete terms what his statement did.

You see, I think we tend to view Christianity through a very narrow lens. We are all products of, and subject to, our cultural and societal norms. To put it simply, we are products of our upbringing. This is even (and perhaps especially) true in religion, though we often fail to recognize it. Or, if we do grasp it, we are reluctant to admit it very loudly. People are listening, you know.

But it must be said: though we cherish the Bible Belt, Christianity is not a southern religion. It's not even an American religion, though to listen to some preachers you would have a hard time believing otherwise.[7]

Christianity is a *universal* religion. A religion for *everyone*. While there may be a million things believers disagree upon, we are united in this: We are disciples of the empty tomb. We join hands with disciples all over the world in confessing that Jesus died for our sins, was buried, and rose again the third day (1 Corinthians 15:3-4). It's the genius of Christianity.

---

[7] If you doubt me, please see the Facebook memes with Jesus and/or the cross proudly draped in the American flag.

An old friend of mine once said he was in search of the one sentence in a literary work that, once read, would fill him with sublimity and transport him to Glory on the spot.

Can a single sentence change you?

I believe so.

**Why I'm Writing**

If I haven't told you by now, I'm a schoolteacher by day. I have a couple of degrees in education. That and a dollar bill will buy you a Coke from most vending machines. It won't change baked lunchroom tater tots into fried ones, and it certainly won't keep my fourth period seventh graders from driving me insane. But most days, it's what I love. And it's what I've done for the last fifteen years.

My current principal recently sent an electronic questionnaire to his teachers. He was new to the job and wanted to know his employees better. One of the last questions on the survey was this:

"Tell me something special or unique about yourself."

That's the question everyone hates. The only thing worse than the question, in my judgment, is the insipid answers it calls forth. "I love Netflix," someone gushes. "I have toes," another relates, blatantly ignoring the "unique" part of the equation.

As for me, I figured I had two options. One was to go the unique-yet-nevertheless-weird route. (And, to be honest, I still can't believe I *didn't* choose this option.) I could have said—so help me, I *started* to say—"I was the three-time spelling bee champion of Calhoun County (1989, 1990, 1991)."[8]

And I really am. Or, at least I was.

Whatever.

But I didn't.

Instead, I went with an utterly annoying, far more pompous sounding, "I have had three books published."

The first book I wrote, back in 2004, was one that a young preacher would write. The kind he thinks will save the world. For some reason, I decided that everyone needed to read that little volume. Consequently, my wife and I sent out 8,632 copies to churches in all fifty states.[9] We followed that up by sending roughly 5,000 copies throughout the community where we lived at the time. I am told by good sources that we basically exhausted what savings we had accrued as a young married couple at the time.[10]

To my chagrin, one gentleman, I believe from New Mexico, sent back a copy of my book with a handwritten note stapled through the front cover. He accused me, if I recall correctly, of "copyrighting the Word of God and trying to sell it for profit." I wondered if it occurred to him that he had received his copy free of charge. It doesn't matter now.

---

[8] I don't know why I was going to supply the years. Just vanity, I suppose.

[9] Not that I counted. Or still have a color-coded map in an old binder to prove it.

[10] Bless Amanda's heart. She never said a word to me about it. Of course, she probably was in shock.

Unless you are Tom Clancy or J.K. Rowling, most writers (and especially writers of religious-themed material) eventually disabuse themselves of the notion that millions of people will read their books.[11] Maybe a few of your friends. May-be. Family? It's a toss-up.

I've mentioned elsewhere that I've apparently lost the ability—or the will—to read lengthy books.[12] I just lose interest. I cannot sustain my focus. Mainly, I get bored. I have the sneaking suspicion that most writers of non-fiction don't say what they really think…they say things that are supposed to sound "writerly"—and it ends up being painfully boring. Or else they say in 300 pages what could easily be said in half that length—or a third.

Not to name names, but I have bought…then sold on Amazon…and years later re-purchased…and again returned…N.T. Wright's massive work *The Resurrection of the Son of God*. It's considered by many scholars to be the magnum opus[13] on the resurrection.

I really wanted to like it.

I thought I was *supposed* to like it.

But it's 817 pages, including the indexes. And the print is small.

---

[11] That reminds me. We had a guy speak to our 7th-12th grade students at a school assembly. A typical motivational-speaker-type who needed psychiatric help himself. On the flier touting his credentials, he boasted of being a "four-time Amazon best-selling author." Out of curiosity, I decided to fact-check him. One of the books he proudly claimed to be a best seller is currently ranked 1,163,197 on Amazon. So there's hope for us all, I guess.

[12] *Do You Know Your Jesus?* Look it up on Amazon, if you're interested.

[13] A Latin term corresponding roughly to, "boring book."

In contrast, Wayne Jackson once described the simple pleasures of reading William Barclay, for instance, as opposed to other writers whom he described as pedantic.[14] I agree.

Though I am not a scholar, nor the son of a scholar, I decided, for better or worse, to write a book that I would want to read. That maybe my kids will read some day. Perhaps a few friends, as well. Who knows.

Because there is so much in life that competes for our attention. So many things that keep us busy. But in quiet moments—and those moments do come, eventually—we are confronted with life's serious questions. About the things that really matter. The only things that matter, if you truly think about it.

This little book is about the most important event in all of history: the resurrection of Jesus Christ from the dead. No matter what you believe on anything else, you must first come to terms with this.

That's what we're going to be talking about, as friends. It's what I want you to think about in quiet moments. And if perchance a little silliness finds its way onto these pages, or perhaps more personal stories than you would prefer, I hope you will forgive me.

There's always N.T. Wright.

---

[14] Pedantic (adjective): (1) Ostentatious in one's learning. (2) Overly concerned with minute details or formalism, especially in teaching.

# Chapter 1

# The Importance of the Resurrection

Some things are just more important than others.

A college basketball game played in March, during the NCAA Tournament, is more important than an intra-squad scrimmage in October. In football, unless you're Alabama[1], you can't expect to lose the last game of the regular season[2], fail to appear in your conference's championship game[3], and still make—much less win—the playoffs.[4] But you can probably lose a game in September and be okay.[5]

**Not All Sin is the Same**

This is also true in matters of religion, although sometimes we forget it.

For example, you will often hear people claim, "All sin is the same." When this is posted on Facebook, three hundred heart emojis instantly appear. (Of course, most people offering this response gave it as much thought as they did the crockpot spam rigatoni recipe they tried from Pinterest.)

---

[1] It happened, kids. Look up the 2017 college football season on Wikipedia.

[2] Auburn 26, Alabama 14.

[3] See also: Alabama 2011.

[4] It wouldn't have mattered anyway. Alabama fans would have claimed the national title regardless.

[5] Applies to all teams except Auburn.

Is all sin really the same?

It certainly is true that all sin is horrible. As James said, "Sin when it is fully grown brings forth death" (1:15). Paul echoed, in a familiar text, "The wages of sin is death" (Romans 6:23).

But that doesn't mean all sin is the *same*.

And we know this, if we think about it a little bit.

Yes, it's wrong to cheat on a test. Even if modern students don't see it that way.

But we typically don't place cheaters in the same category as, say, serial killers.

We make a distinction. Fortunately for seventh graders.

More importantly, Jesus made this distinction.

When Christ was on trial before Pilate, the Roman procurator threatened him: "Do you not know that I have authority to release you and authority to crucify you?" (John 19:10). Jesus responded, "You would have no authority over me at all unless it had been given you from above. Therefore he who delivered me over to you has the greater sin" (John 19:11).

*Greater sin.*

If there is such a thing as "greater sin"—and Christ conceded there is—then by implication, what else must there be?

*Lesser sin.*

That doesn't mean we should rush out to commit all the "little sins" we can—and that's not what Christ said. A "lesser sin" and a "little sin" would be two different things. In fact, it can be argued that there are no "little" sins, given the tremendous price it cost to pay for those sins—the blood of Christ (Acts 20:28).

But the point stands—not all sin is alike.

**Not All Commands are of Equal Weight**

Just so, not all commands in scripture are given the same weight.

During the final week of his earthly ministry Jesus was asked, "Teacher, which is the great commandment in the Law?" (Matthew 22:36).

Christ didn't refuse to answer.

He didn't say, "All commands are equal. Next question."

Instead, he appealed to two texts from the Old Testament, Deuteronomy 6:5 and Leviticus 19:18, in setting forth the cornerstones of religion: love for God and love for neighbor.

This was not the only time the Savior alluded to a potential hierarchy of commands. Later in the same day,[6] Jesus offered a stinging rebuke to the Jewish religious leaders:

"Woe to you, scribes and Pharisees, hypocrites! For you tithe mint and dill and cumin, and have neglected the weightier matters of the law: justice and mercy and

---

[6] Scholars generally recognize this day as Tuesday of the Passion Week.

faithfulness. These you ought to have done, without neglecting the others" (Matthew 23:23).

If there are "heavier" matters—in this case, justice, mercy, and faithfulness—there must also be "lighter" matters. Notice that Jesus did not belittle the lesser things; he stressed obedience to all of God's laws.

But he recognized there is a difference.

**Not All Doctrines are the Same**

If it is the case that not all sins are the same, and if it is also true that not all commands carry equal weight, then it should not be surprising that some theological doctrines are more vital than others.

Again, this does not devalue the intrinsic worth of any Bible teaching. It is not a question of *intrinsic* value, but rather of *comparable* value. Paul recognized this principle when applied to potential converts. All are of equal worth to Christ, in terms of their *souls*. But in their *character* some prove themselves to be "gold," "silver," or "precious stones," while others, who do not stay the course, reveal themselves as "wood," "hay," and "straw" (1 Corinthians 3:12).

The principle of comparative importance may sound strange to us at first, and we may even be inclined to balk at the mention of it, but if we consider it carefully, it should make sense.

For example, "Who wrote the book of Hebrews?" is a frequently asked question concerning the Bible.

I don't know the answer to it. And you don't, either.

In his book *The Case for Jesus*, Brant Pitre quotes the ancient church historian Eusebius, who related that during the second century AD, Origen of Alexandria threw up his hands and declared: "As to who wrote the epistle [to the Hebrews]," only "God knows."[7]

Hebrews is anonymous. God must have wanted it that way for a reason. But surely we can agree that the identity of the *human author* pales in comparison to the *divine message* the book conveys.

And, to build upon this premise, the question "Who wrote the book of Hebrews?" shrinks into virtual insignificance when placed alongside the question, "What must I do to be saved?" (Acts 16:30).

**The Resurrection of Christ: The King of Doctrines**

Which brings us to the resurrection of Jesus.

In the pantheon of Bible doctrines, it can be argued that the resurrection of Christ from the dead occupies the chief seat at the theological table. This may seem like a rather bold claim until it is realized that it also encompasses the divinity of Christ (Romans 1:3-4), the salvation of those who accept it (Romans 10:9; 1 Peter 3:21), and the second coming of the Lord to claim those who belong to him (1 Thessalonians 4:14).

---

[7] Brant Pitre, *The Case for Jesus* (2016), p. 21.

Thus, when you read popular works about the resurrection, it is not uncommon to encounter statements like these:

- "…the Resurrection is the central event in Christianity…"[8]
- "In the war between truth and doubt, nothing outweighs the battle over a certain plot of Jerusalem-area real estate where death moved in on a Friday afternoon and came out the front door big as life on a Sunday morning."[9]
- "…if Christ had not been raised from the dead, then nothing else matters: our resurrection, the church, or Christianity…"[10]

These comments are valuable, as they show the great esteem in which scholars rightly hold the doctrine of the resurrection. But the judgment of the apostle Paul, to continue our theme of comparative importance, surely trumps them all.

Here's the thing.

Paul agrees.

Notice how he begins his great treatise on the resurrection in 1 Corinthians 15.

> Now I would remind you, brothers, of the gospel I preached to you, which you received, in which you stand, and by which you are being saved, if you hold

---

[8] Normal L. Geisler and Frank Turek. *I Don't Have Enough Faith to be An Atheist* (2004), p. 301.

[9] Andreas Kostenberger, Darrel Bock, and Josh Chatraw. *Truth Matters* (2014), p. 160.

[10] Josh McDowell. *Evidence that Demands a Verdict* (2017), p. 236.

fast to the word I preached to you—unless you believed in vain. For I delivered to you as of first importance what I also received: that Christ died for our sins in accordance with the Scriptures, that he was buried, that he was raised on the third day in accordance with the Scriptures…. (vv. 1-4)

Along with his atoning death, Paul described the resurrection of Christ as being "of first importance." In commenting on this passage, Albert Mohler aptly noted:

"All revealed truth is vital, invaluable, life-changing truth to which every disciple of Christ is fully accountable. But certain truths are of highest importance, and that is the language that Paul uses without qualification."[11]

This is precisely what we have been saying. Namely, all truth is God's truth, and all of it is valuable. None of it is unimportant. But some truths occupy the top rung, and the resurrection is chief among them.

## What Is Being Claimed

Perhaps it is good to stop for a moment and state clearly the claim that is being made when we say that Jesus rose from the dead.

There is a hymn we used to sing at the congregation I attended as a child: "I Serve a Risen Savior." The first stanza is as follows:

I serve a risen Savior, He's in the world today;

---

[11] Albert Mohler, "Of First Importance: The Cross and Resurrection at the Center," March 29, 2013. https://albertmohler.com/2013/03/29/of-first-importance-the-cross-and-resurrection-at-the-center-4/

I know that He is living whatever men may say;
I see His hand of mercy, I hear His voice of cheer,
And just the time I need Him, He's always near.

The song concludes with a question, followed by its answer. "You ask me how I know He lives? He lives within my heart."

Please don't misunderstand me. I'm not here to be the song police. These are frustrating individuals to deal with, if you've ever encountered them, and almost always they are wrong.[12] But make no mistake: there are plenty of atheists who would have no problem with this hymn.

"Yes," they would say, "of course it's fine to think that Jesus lives in your heart. But you realize that's the *only* place he lives." This is, in fact, how many liberal theologians justify preaching the resurrection to their congregations, while not believing in it themselves. It is enough for them to subscribe to a "spiritual" resurrection of Christ, in the sense that his example continues to be felt today. But they do not believe, even if their congregants do, that Jesus literally rose from the grave. That is the stuff of make-believe, they would say.

Listen. I've had pets over the years that I have cherished. My first dog, a dachshund named Rusty. Gizmo, a Shih

---

[12] I once had a gentleman tell me, for example, that it was inappropriate to sing the traditional Lord's Supper hymn, "Lead Me to Calvary." His reasoning? The song begins, "King of my life, I crown thee now…" He said, "Jesus is our King, whether we crown him or not." Of course that is true. But he forgot, I suppose, Paul's statement that God "is the Savior of all people, especially of those who believe" (1 Timothy 4:10). Although God is the Father of mankind, he has a special relationship with those who are his own. The song police strike out again.

Tzu we named during the Gremlin craze of the 1980s.[13] I have fond memories of these and other pets I've owned. You might even say that some of them continue to live within my heart.[14] But in no sense do I believe these pets are literally alive today, continuing to enjoy a conscious, actual existence.

But I do believe that about Jesus.

When I sing about him, not only do I proclaim that he lives within my heart, but I also believe that he is literally alive, even now, and occupies a real body. Indeed, as Jesus said himself, "I died, and behold, I am alive forevermore" (Revelation 1:18).

The Christian belief is that Jesus of Nazareth was an actual person who lived in history. He was born in Bethlehem during the reign of Augustus (27 BC-AD 14) and was crucified during the reign of Tiberius (AD 14-37). Although he was a living, breathing human being, he was more. Jesus was God in the flesh (John 1:14), who gave his life for the sins of the world (1 John 2:2). Although he died as a result of crucifixion on a Friday in AD 30 around 3 pm, by the following Sunday morning he had risen physically from the grave.

---

[13] Gizmo met his untimely demise while we were away on our trip to Disney World in 1985, the victim of a hit and run. Not a good way to come home from the Happiest Place in the World.

[14] We had two cats when my family lived in Trussville, Alabama, and later in Ashville: Thomas and Jackson. Thomas was named for Thomas B. Warren, who debated the noted atheist Antony G.N. Flew. Jackson was named for Wayne Jackson. Both men were faithful gospel preachers (but not the cats, who sadly apostatized). My son, Jackson, is also named for Wayne Jackson. I may have mentioned that elsewhere.

The resurrected Christ was not merely a phantom, as he testified himself. "See my hands and my feet, that it is I myself. Touch me, and see. For a spirit does not have flesh and bones as you see that I have" (Luke 24:39).

Jesus is real.

As James Packer noted, "Jesus is not just a historical memory, one who is dead yet speaks as model and mentor, like Abel, but he is a living Savior, a loving Master, and an everlasting friend to all who trust him."[15]

## The "No Resurrection" Consequences

Why should **you** be interested in the resurrection of Jesus Christ?

After all, isn't this just a philosophical discussion for preacher-types who have too much time on their hands? An exercise in theological gymnastics that has no real bearing on reality?

No.

In fact, the stakes could not be any higher.

In Paul's day, there were some Christians in Greece who were flirting with the idea that there would be no bodily resurrection from the grave. The general Greek conception of the body was that it essentially was evil. At best, it was an embarrassment. To be free from the body, to be purely a spirit, was considered the highest form of release. If this

---

[15] Quoted in Gary Habermas and Antony Flew. *Did Jesus Rise From The Dead? The Resurrection Debate* (1987), p. 143.

was so, then why would anyone desire a bodily existence in the afterlife?

When some in the Corinthian church adopted this idea, and began to propagate it, Paul addressed their error in no uncertain terms.

The first thing he did was to link the believers' future resurrection with that of Christ's. Notice his statement in 1 Corinthians 15:13:

"But if there is no resurrection of the dead, then not even Christ has been raised."

It seems the Corinthians had not yet denied the resurrection of Jesus. But Paul wanted them to understand that their resurrection was tied so closely with Christ's that to reject one was to reject the other. In other words, if they were going to claim there was no future resurrection—and a bodily one, at that, which was the point in contention—then they might as well argue that Jesus did not rise from the dead. Surely, they were not willing to go that far.

Conversely, if they were willing to accept that Jesus rose bodily from the grave, they should also agree that they would rise in bodily fashion, as well. Their respective resurrections (the Corinthians' and that of Christ) stood or fell together, as it were.

Perhaps the Corinthians had not fully considered the implications of the "no resurrection" doctrine. If that was the case, Paul was happy to spell them out.

If there was to be no bodily resurrection of the dead, then:

1.  Not even Christ has been raised (v. 13)
2.  The apostles' preaching was in vain (v. 14)
3.  The Corinthians' faith was in vain (v. 14)
4.  The apostles were misrepresenting God (v. 15)
5.  Not even Christ has been raised (v. 16—he repeats himself for emphasis)
6.  The Corinthians' faith was futile (v. 17—another essential repetition)
7.  The Corinthians were still in their sins (v. 17)
8.  Those who had fallen asleep in Christ had perished (v. 17)

Given these dire alternatives, is there any wonder Paul would say, "If in Christ we have hope in this life only, we are of all people most to be pitied" (1 Corinthians 15:19). The apostle sounded a similarly bleak note, later in the same treatise: "If the dead are not raised, 'Let us eat and drink, for tomorrow we die'" (1 Corinthians 15:32).[16]

## Christ: The Firstfruits

Had Paul ended his remarks in 1 Corinthians 15:19, the situation would have appeared bleak indeed.

No future resurrection, no forgiveness, no hope.

Nothing—but despair.

But the apostle didn't stop there.

---

[16] I have heard preachers say over the years, "Even if Christianity weren't true, it would still be the best life to live." That's not what Paul said. If there is no resurrection, to live the Christian life would be to live a lie—something no right-thinking person would want to do.

Notice verse 20:

"But in fact Christ has been raised from the dead, the firstfruits of those who have fallen asleep."

Paul is employing harvest imagery from the Old Testament. The feast of firstfruits was closely connected with the observance of the Passover, as it was celebrated during the same week (Leviticus 23:9ff).

The "firstfruits" were just what the name implies: "Some of the first of all the fruit of the ground" (Deuteronomy 26:2). The fruit was placed in a basket and given to the priest, who then placed it on the altar before Jehovah. It was offered in gratitude for previous blessings, and in confidence that God would continue to provide the Israelites' every need. It was, in a very real sense, a faith pledge of the full harvest to come.

In 1 Corinthians 5:7, Paul writes: "For Christ, our Passover lamb, has been sacrificed." The death of the first Passover lambs, along with the smearing of their blood on the doorposts and lintel, had spared the Israelites from the Destroyer (Exodus 12:1ff). Paul sees the ultimate fulfillment of this imagery in the death of Christ: because of the Savior's sacrifice, our sins have been forgiven, covered by his blood. As Paul elsewhere relates, we are therefore "saved by him from the wrath of God" (Romans 5:9).

The connection is irresistible: If Christ's death is the Christian's Passover, then his resurrection is the firstfruits. The two are inseparable. Just as the two feasts were linked in the Old Testament—overlapping, as it were[17]—they remain connected today. It's quite remarkable, really.

To think of it another way: If the death of Christ was the *payment* for our sins, his resurrection is the believer's *receipt*—that is, it is the guarantee of a future bodily resurrection in the age to come. This is precisely what Paul meant by describing Christ as the "firstfruits" in 1 Corinthians 15:20.

Since Jesus was raised, everyone will be raised.

He was the firstfruits—we are the "harvest" that will follow.

It's guaranteed. You can take it to the bank.

**We Will Be Like Jesus**

Not only does Christ's resurrection afford the assurance that we will be raised, it is also, as Paul argued to the Corinthians, the guarantee that you will (eventually) have a body in eternity. You cannot separate the two ideas— namely, a resurrection means a body.

Indeed, whatever view of the final abode you subscribe to, you will have a body there.

It is certainly true, as Ecclesiastes 12:7 teaches, that at death the spirit returns to God, while the body returns to dust. Hebrews 12:23 also makes mention of "the spirits of

---

[17] The Passover feast began at twilight on the 14th day of the Jewish month Nisan and lasted for a week. The Feast of Firstfruits took place on the 16th of Nisan.

the righteous made perfect" worshiping around the throne of God.

But the resurrection is coming.

And, as Tim Keller has noted:

> Unlike the Greek religions and the pagan religions and the Eastern religions, Christians do not envision a "bodyless" eternity. We don't see the body as a bad thing at all. No. God created my body and my soul and he's going to redeem my body and my soul.[18]

A redeemed body paired with a redeemed soul.

A body that experiences no pain, is subject neither to death nor decay, and is as immortal as that of Christ's (Revelation 21:4).

A body freed from fleshly temptations (1 John 2:17), unhindered by physical limitations (John 20:19), able to accomplish whatever the mind and heart of God has prepared for it to do. "A spiritual body"—a body fitted for the world to come—as Paul described it in 1 Corinthians 15:44.

It is incredible to think about, as little as we presently can fathom it.

But it is the plain and unflinching teaching of the Bible.

"When Christ appears, we shall be like him" (1 John 3:2).

---

[18] Tim Keller (1991). Sermon: "I Am the Resurrection and the Life." New York City: Redeemer Presbyterian Church.

Jesus "will transform our lowly body to be like his glorious body" (Philippians 3:21).

All of this, "not because of works done by us in righteousness" (Titus 3:5), but because Jesus Christ rose from the dead on our behalf.

He "was delivered up for our trespasses and raised for our justification" (Romans 4:25).

Truly, he was raised to save us.

Praise his holy name.

# Chapter 2
# Defending the Resurrection

"What are you reading, dad?" asked Jackson, my son.

He was six years old at the time.

"I'm reading *The Case for the Resurrection of Jesus.*"

"Hmmm…" he said. "I thought you were going to say the butler did it."

He comes by it honestly.[1]

For as long as I can remember, I've had an interest in defending the truth. Wendell Winkler shared this passion, once admitting that when he was a young preacher, he had "a mania about error."

I can relate to that.

When I was a young man, I subscribed to brotherhood periodicals that dealt with the latest religious controversies, ranging from what Bible version was being used in our pulpits to whether women should function as translators in overseas missions.

I even wrote for some of those publications.[2]

---

[1] When I told Jack I was writing this book, he said, "I don't believe it." Why, son? "Mainly because I didn't know you could read." I'm going to have to have a long talk with that boy, some day.

[2] All evidence of these crimes has long since been destroyed.

It's probably a personality trait.

Even now, I struggle mightily against the inclination to critique what I perceive as intellectual errors.[3] The urge to say, "What are you thinking?" can be overwhelming at times.[4] Sometimes I yield to it, if only in my mind.[5]

This is not a bad thing.

Not entirely.

Because some error *needs* correcting.

Paul certainly felt that way, as we noted in the previous chapter, when he admonished the Corinthians about the resurrection.

Because—as is true of sin, commands, and doctrines—not all error is the same, either.

In addition to their resurrection questions, some in Corinth had been perplexed about eating meat that had been offered to idols. Should they partake or should they abstain?

Provided their conscience was pure (and no easily offended brethren were around), it really didn't matter. As Paul told them, "Food will not commend us to God. We

---

[3] Who am I kidding? I struggle to keep my mouth shut during faculty meetings. My personal favorite is when teachers, at the end a lengthy session, ask questions that apply only to themselves. "Mr. Laney, an aardvark is eating bologna in my front yard. What should I do?" (Clay-Chalkville High School faculty meeting, circa 2008).

[4] It is amazing that I have any friends. Wait a minute…never mind.

[5] Or, if the stupidity is deserving enough, with an ill-advised Facebook comment.

are no worse off if we do not eat, and no better off if we do" (1 Corinthians 8:8).

The resurrection, though…the resurrection was a totally different matter. It had to be defended, regardless of how the Greek culture felt about "bodies." Rather than capitulate for the sake of the uninformed, Paul instead lobbed this warning their way:

"Do not be deceived: 'Bad company ruins good morals'" (1 Corinthians 15:33).

In other words, they had better take careful stock as to who or what was shaping their theological framework: God's word or the Greek culture at large.

Paul pulled no punches: the resurrection must be safeguarded from attack, whether from within the body of Christ or from without.

**The Empty Tomb**

Which brings us to the most hallowed real estate of all in this discussion:

The empty tomb.

As Kostenberger, Bock, and Chatraw[6] relate in *Truth Matters*:

---

[6] Do you see why you should never have three authors for a single work, without distinguishing who wrote what? In citing the book you sound like you're quoting a law firm. Have you been injured in an accident? Call Kostenberger, Bock, and Chatraw for all your legal needs.

Whatever theory makes the most sense to skeptics on any given day, their chosen model must at least involve the reality of an opened grave. Because when the story began circulating in the hours following Jesus' death, suggesting that he had been miraculously raised from the dead, one quick swing out to his final resting place would have been the only, simple, falling-off-a-log requirement to stop all this fanatical discussion. One body meant no story.[7]

But no one in the first century, so far as we know, ever claimed to find the body of Jesus.

And no archaeological expedition since then has uncovered his remains.

Whether one is a fervent believer or a just-as-passionate skeptic, this truth must be admitted:

*The tomb was empty.*

## Evidence-Based Faith

When I was growing up, as silly as it may sound, the objection that bothered me the most when it came to religious matters was, "How do you know?"

The scenario would go something like this. You'd state your belief on a given topic, which you had studied carefully to develop, only to have someone who had given it little thought, by comparison, question you.

It bugged me. It probably was a pride thing.

---

[7] *Truth Matters*, p. 161.

In time I learned that this is not a bad question.

Nor is it unfair to ask.

Because after all, it's only a question.

It's not an argument. It's not even an assertion.

It's just a question.[8]

It may be a legitimate request for information. Or, as I suspect in many cases, it may be an attempt to push back a little, albeit weakly.

I think the answer that I would give today would go something like this: "What does the evidence suggest?"

Evidence. That's what wins the day.

Far from conflicting with faith, evidence undergirds faith.

As the Hebrews writer related, "Now faith is the substance of things hoped for, the evidence of things not seen" (Hebrews 11:1, KJV). The ESV renders it like this: "Now faith is the assurance of things hoped for, the conviction of things not seen."

Our faith, then, is a conviction—a conviction based on evidence. Walking "by faith, not by sight" (2 Corinthians 5:7) does not mean stumbling blindly in the dark. It means, in the present case, that while we did not see the actual events of resurrection morning unfold, we are not without historical witness.

---

[8] Do I sound like I'm trying to convince myself?

## The Known Historical Facts

With apologies (again) to N.T. Wright, it probably is correct to say that the world's foremost expert on the resurrection of Christ is Gary Habermas.

In his many debates on this issue, Habermas typically begins with what he calls "the minimal facts." These are items that most scholars, regardless of their religious (or irreligious) persuasion, generally agree upon.

One list Habermas makes frequent use of includes these twelve facts.[9]

1. Jesus died by crucifixion.
2. He was buried.
3. The death of Jesus caused the disciples to despair and lose hope, believing that his life had ended.
4. The tomb in which Jesus was buried was discovered to be empty just a few days later.
5. The disciples had experiences they believed were the literal appearances of the risen Jesus.
6. The disciples were transformed from doubters who were afraid to identify themselves with Jesus to bold proclaimers of his death and resurrection.
7. This message was the center of preaching in the early church.
8. This message was especially proclaimed in Jerusalem, where Jesus died and was buried.
9. As a result of this teaching, the church was born and grew.
10. Sunday became the primary day of worship.

---

[9] *Did the Resurrection Happen?*, pp. 22-23.

11.  James, who had been a skeptic, was converted to the faith when he also believed that he had seen the resurrected Jesus.

12.  A few years later, Paul was converted by an experience that he likewise believed to be an appearance of the risen Jesus.

The genius of this approach, as Habermas contends, is that it does not depend on what one believes about the Bible in order to be valid. In other words, these are brute historical facts, whatever one's view of inspiration, or of the Bible in general. As believers, we trust that the Bible is the inspired Word of God. Skeptics, of course, do not share in that view.

With the known historical facts model, one's view of inspiration is rendered moot. Or, if you prefer, it is set aside for the time being. To borrow from Captain Jack Ross in *A Few Good Men*, "These are the facts of the case, and they are undisputed."[10]

But I can see someone with her hand raised already.

"If these facts are so agreed upon, then why doesn't everyone accept the resurrection of Jesus?"

Aye, there's the rub.[11]

People reject the resurrection for a variety of reasons, not all of them intellectual—and none of them logical, in the

---

[10] There is probably a joke here about six degrees of separation from Kevin Bacon to the resurrection of Jesus, but I, for one, will not be guilty of making it.

[11] This is something William Shakespeare once wrote in *Hamlet*. No one probably understood it then, and no one understands it now. I'm told it means, "Here's the catch."

end. Some individuals had no religious upbringing, and consequently were never exposed to the teaching.[12] Others have been unduly influenced by naturalism and contend that miracles are impossible by definition.[13] A third category intrigues me but is especially unfortunate: those who rebelled at a bad religious upbringing[14] and pretend to posit intellectual reasons for what really is an emotional problem.

We won't go into any of these just yet. But you need to be prepared for the fact that not everyone will immediately accept the resurrection, just because you showed them a few facts most scholars believe to be true.

Don't let this discourage you, though, as it once did me.

After Paul set forth an airtight case for the bodily resurrection, he knew there still would be objections. "But some man will say…" (1 Corinthians 15:35).

Yes, they will.

---

[12] And, it must be admitted, some who enjoyed a religious upbringing accept the resurrection blindly, never having given it much critical thought. Both groups, it turns out, either accept or reject the resurrection ignorantly. Neither attitude is commendable.

[13] They would argue somewhat like this: (1) Nothing happens outside of nature; (2) The resurrection of Jesus would be outside of nature; (3) Therefore, the resurrection of Jesus did not happen. The problem lies with the major premise—that nature is all there is. As Frank Turek argues in *Stealing From God,* since nature had a beginning, nature can't be its own cause. There must be something *outside* of nature. When someone objected to this by claiming that in time a natural cause will be discovered for nature, Turek responded: "That's like saying, 'Give me more time and I'll discover that I gave birth to my own mother!' It's impossible in principle" (p. 4).

[14] In other words, they may have been taught the truth, per se, but it was not modeled and grounded in love. The adage about "preachers' kids" is a cliché, to be sure, but it's a cliché for a reason.

And what will we say, in response?

Here's what we'll say. We'll sound so smart.[15]

"What's the most reasonable interpretation of the available evidence?"

(And if that doesn't work, we'll just use Paul's rejoinder: "You foolish person!")

**The Resurrection Creed**

One of the strongest historical arguments for the resurrection of Jesus is the so-called "resurrection creed," found in 1 Corinthians 15:3-7.

> For I delivered to you as of first importance what I also received: that Christ died for our sins in accordance with the Scriptures, that he was buried, that he was raised on the third day in accordance with the Scriptures, and that he appeared to Cephas, then to the twelve. Then he appeared to more than five hundred brothers at one time, most of whom are still alive, though some have fallen asleep. Then he appeared to James, then to all the apostles.

Paul wrote the letter we call "1 Corinthians" sometime between AD 55-57. Since it generally is conceded that Christ was crucified in AD 30,[16] that would mean Paul was writing a quarter of a century after the original events occurred. As anyone who has studied history knows, this

---

[15] Or like a jerk. You have to be careful.

[16] Some scholars believe AD 33.

is an incredibly *short* gap of time when it comes to chronicling ancient events.

But we can get even closer to the actual events than this.

Notice Paul says he "delivered" what he had "received." These words—"delivered" and "received"—are "technical rabbinic words [used] for passing on a tradition."[17] In fact, for these and other reasons, scholars believe that Paul is referring to a specific creed[18] he had received on a previous occasion.

But when? And under what circumstances?

Paul's conversion is thought to have been just two years after the death of Jesus. If Christ was crucified in AD 30, this would mean Paul became a Christian around AD 32.

Not long afterwards, the apostle made a trip to Jerusalem, during which he visited with Peter and with James, the Lord's brother. He references this trip in Galatians 1:18: "Then after three years I went up to Jerusalem to visit Cephas and remained with him fifteen days."

Adding three years to AD 32 brings us to AD 35—just *five years* after the resurrection.

But we can go even further back into history.

The material Paul had "received" and now was "delivering" to the Corinthians was conveyed to him by

---

[17] David Baggett, quoted in *Did Jesus Rise From the Dead?*, p. 115.

[18] A creed is simply something that is believed. It is a perfectly neutral term, though it has come to have solely negative connotations in some quarters. What you believe is your creed. We all have a creed.

eyewitnesses to the actual events, pushing the creed all the way back to the very events it chronicled. As David Baggett notes, "For the historian, this sort of evidence is nothing less than golden."[19]

For some believers, this approach might seem unnecessary. After all, did not the apostle Paul write by inspiration? Of course he did (1 Corinthians 14:37). But inspiration did not free him from doing his due diligence in gathering whatever relevant information he could obtain. Was this not the same method Luke employed, in writing his Gospel and Acts (Luke 1:3)?

Remember, Gary Habermas is making a purely historical case, regardless of one's view of inspiration. And what evidence is he putting forth?

That of the eyewitnesses.

In this text alone (1 Corinthians 15:3-7), Paul mentions:

- Cephas (Peter)
- The Twelve
- More than 500 brothers at one time
- James
- The apostles

Paul then alludes to himself, of course, "as to one untimely born" (v. 8).

What's the point? Here's the point.

---

[19] *Did Jesus Rise From the Dead?*, p. 115.

Many of these individuals were *still alive* when Paul wrote (1 Corinthians 15:6), and *therefore could be interviewed.* How could Paul have penned such a document, which was intended to be read in public, if what he was saying was not, in fact, true?

It would have been intellectual suicide—character suicide—career suicide—of the first degree.

He would have been laughed out of court. Run out of town on a rail.

Had it not been true.

Every bit of it.

**Alternate Explanations**

Still, even in the face of powerful evidence, there are those who refuse to be persuaded. Their challenge is to come up with an alternate explanation for the empty tomb that is just as plausible as the one they are rejecting—namely, that Christ rose from the grave.

We will notice a few of the commonly offered explanations and make brief responses to each.

**The Swoon Theory**

This skeptical theory was largely abandoned in the 1800s.[20] And for good reason.

This was the notion that Jesus did not actually die on the cross, but rather "swooned," a rather antiquated way of

---

[20] *Did Jesus Rise From the Dead?,* p. 69.

saying that Jesus passed out. In other words, after enduring a brutal beating by the Romans, followed by a six-hour crucifixion ordeal, Jesus later revived in a damp, dark tomb, managed to force his way out, remove the massive stone that covered the opening, get past the armed guards, and convince his disciples that he had risen from the dead.

Had any of this been possible, the disciples likely would have said: "You may be alive, but you're certainly not risen. Let's get you to a doctor!"[21]

**The Wrong Tomb Debacle**

Others believe that the disciples simply went to the wrong tomb on the morning of the resurrection. Finding it empty, they mistakenly concluded that Christ had returned from the dead.[22]

Do you see several problems with this? For one thing, if the disciples had gone to the wrong tomb, the Romans and/or the Jews quickly would have gone to the right tomb, and the matter would have ended there.[23] "See, there he is!" Case closed.

In truth, this theory reminds me more of an old Abbott and Costello routine than a serious response. Did *everyone* suddenly forget where they had buried Jesus—just hours before? The tomb belonged to a prominent Jewish man (Matthew 27:60). It was guarded by Romans (Matthew

---

[21] *I Don't Have Enough Faith to be an Atheist*, p. 305.

[22] Who, finding an empty tomb, would immediately conclude, "They must be risen from the dead!" It was more than the empty tomb that led to the disciples' belief in the resurrection. Paul himself was not convinced by the empty tomb alone. It took the appearance(s) of the risen Savior.

[23] *I Don't Have Enough Faith to be an Atheist*, p. 302.

27:66). Several women had watched intently as the Lord's body was entombed there (Luke 23:55). As William Lane Craig noted, and as Geisler and Turek relate, this theory suggests that everyone involved developed "a permanent kind of collective amnesia about what they had done with the body of Jesus."[24]

There's one last problem with this idea—and it's a big one. The "wrong tomb" theory also fails to account for the subsequent appearances of the risen Christ, at least twelve in all.[25] As Geisler and Turek observe, it's not enough merely to develop a theory to account for the empty tomb. One also must explain the resurrection appearances. This theory, as they note, accomplishes neither.[26]

## The Hallucination Theory

In his three debates with Habermas, Antony Flew was inclined to argue that the post-resurrection appearances of Jesus were mere hallucinations on the part of Christ's followers. The disciples were so grief stricken, it is claimed, they conjured up visions of the risen Savior from the depths of their broken hearts.

---

[24] Quoted in Ibid., p. 303.

[25] (1) To Mary Magdalene (John 20:10ff); (2) To Mary Magdalene and the other Mary (Matthew 28:1ff); (3) To Peter (1 Corinthians 15:5) and John (John 20:1ff); (4) To two disciples (Luke 24:13ff); (5) To ten apostles (Luke 24:36-49; John 20:19-23); (6) To eleven apostles (John 20:24-31); (7) To seven apostles (John 21); (8) To all the apostles (Matthew 28:16-20; Mark 16:14-18); (9) To 500 people (1 Corinthians 15:6); (10) To James (1 Corinthians 15:7); (11) To all the apostles (Acts 1:4-8); (12) To Paul (Acts 9:1-9; 1 Corinthians 15:8). Adapted from *I Don't Have Enough Faith to be an Atheist*, p. 303.

[26] *I Don't Have Enough Faith to be an Atheist*, p. 304.

As with the previous theories, the problems with the hallucination hypothesis are many and grievous.

First, the disciples were not expecting to see the risen Jesus. He was, in fact, the last person they thought they would see. He was dead, and, so far as they believed, he would stay that way. When Mary of Magdalene saw the risen Savior, she did not say, "I've been expecting you." Instead, she mistook him for the gardener (John 20:15).

Second, Jesus appeared to over 500 different individuals, on at least twelve different occasions. Was everyone experiencing the *same* hallucination? As Habermas pointed out to Flew, "Group appearances are very difficult for hallucinations, because we don't hallucinate the same thing together."[27]

Third, the hallucination theory also fails to account for the empty tomb. If the visions of the risen Christ were nothing more than wishful thinking, the authorities could have gone to the tomb, produced the body of Jesus, and ended the "dream" of Christianity on the spot. But they didn't. Because the body was not there.

## The Conspiracy Theory

Finally, some have argued that the disciples hastily conspired to steal the body of Jesus. Having accomplished their nefarious plan, they then claimed that Christ was alive from the dead and were able to launch the incredible movement we know of as Christianity.

---

[27] *Did the Resurrection Happen?*, p. 41.

There are so many holes with this theory, it's hard to know where to begin. Perhaps the best reply is simply to make an appeal to human nature. While it's true that some people are willing to die for what they believe is the truth, very few are willing to die for what they *know* is a lie. Somewhere along the line, the weakest link in the chain eventually will break.

And yet the disciples never broke. They never recanted their story. They never turned "State's evidence." They chose to be imprisoned, tortured, and killed rather than give up the great "hoax" they had perpetrated. It doesn't pass the smell test.

Tim Keller once shared this excellent quote from Blaise Pascal: "I believe those witnesses who get their throats cut." To this, Keller added: "Virtually all the apostles and early Christian leaders died for their faith, and it is hard to believe that this kind of powerful self-sacrifice would be done to support a hoax."[28]

## All You Can Do Is Laugh

There are other explanations offered in the attempt to explain away the empty tomb, but they are no more persuasive than any we've noticed. Islam teaches, for example, that a "stand-in" for Christ died on the cross, and not the real Jesus. Well, was the tomb of the stand-in also found empty on the third day? Did he, too, rise from the dead?

Bible scholar J.W. McGarvey lived a long time ago.

---

[28] *The Reason for God*, p. 218.

But he knew just what to do in these situations. Listen to him.

> ...some things are exposed in their nakedness as soon as you turn the laugh on them, and a good laugh is sometimes more effective than any amount of argument. If a fellow should stand up and say that two and two make five, and you should undertake to argue with him, such a fellow will dispute all day, and have the last word in spite of you. But if you laugh, the company will probably laugh with you, and that's an end of the matter.[29]

## The Burden of Proof

It's customary for those who reject the resurrection to claim, "The burden of proof is on you"—meaning the onus is on the believer to offer his reasons.

That is correct.

And it's what we've done in this chapter.

But it's not the end of the story.

And they don't get off the hook that easily.

It's not enough for the unbeliever to say, "Nope. Don't believe it. End of story."

They also have a burden of proof, whether they realize it or not.

---

[29] *Short Essays in Biblical Criticism*, pp. 72-73.

Their task is to explain how, if the resurrection never occurred, the Christian church nevertheless exploded onto the scene, an overnight "Big Bang," as it were—not only surviving persecution but flourishing in the face of it.

What led thousands of Jews—strict monotheists[30]—to come to believe that a human being (Jesus) was worthy of their worship? The Jews had certainly lapsed into idolatry earlier in their history, but they never worshiped mere men. Never.

How to account for this—if not for the resurrection of Jesus?

**A Final Word**

We may not be able to convince everyone that Jesus Christ rose from the dead.

In fact, it's quite certain that we won't.

But that doesn't mean we shouldn't try.

Nor does it mean we lack solid historical evidence.

We close this chapter with the words of Wolfhart Pannenberg.[31]

> There are good and even superior reasons for claiming that the Resurrection of Jesus was a historical event, and consequently the risen Lord

---

[30] Believers in one God.

[31] If I had a nickel for every time I've quoted Wolfhart Pannenberg…I'd have a nickel. Still, it feels like a special moment, and one not likely to be replicated by this writer. I'm glad you were here to share it with me.

himself is a living reality. And yet there is the innumerably repeated experience that in this world the dead do not rise again. As long as this is the case, the Christian affirmation of Jesus' Resurrection will remain a debated issue, in spite of all the sound historical argument as to its historicity. Although Christians should never lose their nerve in this matter but insist on the historicity of Jesus' Resurrection as long as the evidence warrants such a claim, they also should not be surprised that only in the kingdom to come, when the dead rise again, will the opposition to their claim vanish.[32]

---

[32] *Did Jesus Rise From the Dead?*, pp. 134-135.

# Chapter 3
# Living Out the Resurrection

**A Tale of Whimsy**

Everyone has stories they like to tell.

And re-tell.

As for me? I might have a couple.

If you have a minute, I'll tell you one.

For the rest of you, who know full well that the story of an angry geriatric substitute teacher has no place in a book on the resurrection of Christ, I recommend that you skip immediately to the next heading.

I must caution you, though.

It's about the Misfit.


[First Intermission]


You're still here?

Then let us begin.

When I was in first grade, there was a substitute teacher we thought was ancient. Chances are, she was in her late sixties. But when you're seven, anyone over thirty is practically in the throes of death.

One day, our regular teacher was absent. And, instead of having the Ancient Substitute, we had the Mother of the Ancient Substitute.

I kid you not.

Our heads spun. We were temporarily stunned. Even now, with advanced carbon dating methods, I have to believe this woman was in her mid-eighties, easily.

As we strained to establish common ground with this pedagogical octogenarian,[1] a classmate, Tony Heath, blurted out something that would live in infamy, if only in my mind.

"Mrs. Acker, Brandon knows everything!"

In my defense, I never claimed omniscience.

I never even hinted at it, as best I can recall.

I knew a few facts about U.S. presidents, sure, from having an early interest in our nation's history. I liked old baseball players, too. My dad bought me a few reprints of the Hall of Famers that I pored over religiously. As a result, I could regale my elders[2] with tales of Mordecai "Three Finger" Brown, who, despite losing parts of two

---

[1] A needlessly wordy way of saying, "old teacher." Just figured I'd never have the chance to use that exact phrase again.
[2] Mainly my brother and his friends.

fingers in a nasty farming accident, would develop an even nastier curveball and go on to win 239 big league games.

But enough about the three-fingered wonder.

Because, as I feel was probably true with most things in her life, Mrs. Acker was not impressed.

Instead, she went on the offensive.

"Okay, young man. What year was George Washington born?"

Well, it just so happened that George Washington was a president that I had read about. In fact, I once checked out a book that had the audacity to claim that Washington lost more battles in his military career than he won. This enraged my sense of patriotism. Against all proper decorum—and consider this my confession to the Piedmont Public Librarian—I took an ink pen and marked through those traitorous lines, changing it instead to read, "Won more battles than he lost."

It was my duty to my country.

At any rate, I answered Mrs. Acker, perhaps a bit too eagerly.

"1732."

Now, what *should* Mrs. Acker have said to me at this point?

"Wow! That's very impressive knowledge for a first grader. Well done!"

But, I'm sorry to tell you, that is *not* what Mrs. Acker said to me.

The woman would not be denied.

She continued a full-frontal assault.

"Okay, then. What year did he *die*?"

To my credit, I saw where this was headed.[3]

I knew, for reasons detailed above, that our beloved first president met his Maker in 1799.

But I also knew that this Gestapo holdover would not relent until finally I broke. Rather than continue with the quizzical Inquisition, I did something I know I should not have done.

I lied.

"Gosh, I don't know when George Washington died."[4]

Anyone with a working heart—and any remnant of a soul—knows *exactly* what Mrs. Acker should have said to me at this juncture of the verbal repartee.

"Well, that's okay. It's still *fantastic* that you knew the year of his birth. Most *adults* don't know that information."

But, I'm sorry to tell you, that is *not* what she said.

---

[3] Note to self: First graders are more perceptive than you think.

[4] I'm pretty sure I didn't use the mild euphemism here. It just sounds like what Opie Taylor would have said to Mrs. Crump.

What she said was this.

"Hmph. Nobody likes a know-it-all."[5]

Oh, how I wish I could go back in time, and tell seven-year-old-me not to kowtow[6] to this browbeating Nazi.[7] To keep going…to answer all her presidential questions in rapid-fire fashion…until she was forced to collapse into her easy chair, riddled with defeat.

Or maybe I should just tell Young Brandon not to lie.

It's a moral dilemma, really.

When I tell my students this story today, they usually laugh.

Those with greater perception marvel at the degree of callousness of this dark, evil woman.

"Where is she now?" they often ask.

"I'm not sure," is all I can manage to say.

---

[5] I wish technology was such that even in the print version of this book, as soon as your eyes encountered the words "know-it-all," the font would change to a size 300, with the words also reverberating several times in your ears. "Know it all" … "Know it all" … "KNOW IT ALL." Because that was roughly the effect it had on me.

[6] Word of the day: Kowtow (verb): To act in a fawning manner; show servile deference.

[7] Too harsh? I think not. She had a slightly faded swastika tattooed to her bicep. (So not true.)

## "The Misfit": How Jesus Changes Everything

If you decided to skip over the preceding tale of whimsy, I don't blame you in the slightest.

What I really wanted to tell you starts here, anyway.

Here it is.

Timothy Keller is one of my favorite preachers in the world.

He's not a bad writer, either.

And he has a story that he'd like to tell you.

Believe me, he does.

Whenever Keller discourses on the resurrection—or on any subject, really—there's a better than average chance he will reference one of two writers:

C.S. Lewis or Flannery O'Connor.

Most likely, he will reference Lewis, the celebrated British author and Christian apologist.

But when the time is right, Keller will allude to what he calls his "favorite short story, a peerless story"—O'Connor's "A Good Man Is Hard to Find."

The story, as you may know, revolves around the Misfit, an escaped convict who terrorizes an unsuspecting family.

I'll let Keller tell you the story in his own words, as he once told them in a sermon at Redeemer Presbyterian

Church, in New York City.[8] (Remember he's speaking, not writing—or you'll have second thoughts about the whole "good writer" stuff.)

> The Misfit has captured a family and needs the car, so he is taking the family members one at a time into the woods and killing them. As he's doing this, he's talking to the grandmother, the matron of the clan. The grandmother represents all the shallowness of our human culture because she keeps on saying to him, as his henchmen take the little boys and girls off into the woods and shoot them, "I can tell you're a good man. You wouldn't do this. You wouldn't harm people. Yeah, I can tell you're a good man."
>
> Just before the Misfit shoots her three times in the chest, he basically says to her, "Hey, there are no good and bad people. Instead, Jesus has thrown everything off balance. If he did what he said, then there is nothing to do but to throw away everything and follow him, and if he didn't, then there is nothing to do than enjoy the few minutes you have left by killing someone or burning down his house or doing some meanness, and there is hardly no pleasure in that."

How perfect! Do you see what he's saying? He says, "What's this good and bad stuff? If Jesus Christ is who he said he was, that's one thing. If there is no Jesus Christ or if he is not God, if we can't know God personally through him, or if we don't know if there

---

8 Tim Keller (1990). "New Life," Sermon delivered at Redeemer Presbyterian Church, October 14, 1990.

is a God and we have no hope and we're not sure about these things, then who's to say what's good? Who's to say what's kind? Who's to say what's courageous? If I want to shoot people, who's going to say that's wrong?"

He says, "On the other hand, if Jesus was who he said he was then we have to throw everything over and follow him. If there's Jesus then we have a reason for following him, and if he's not who he said he was then nobody has a right to talk about right or wrong or good or bad."

Don't you see? Your very life hinges on the answer to the question, "Who is Jesus?" Everybody in this room, everybody in this town, either responsibly or irresponsibly, either without any kind of decent reflection or with reflection, has made the decision, and that decision has completely affected how they live. The Misfit was right.

Perhaps I should've warned you, if you didn't know already, that O'Connor's stories were famed for their grotesque elements.

But O'Connor was right. Even if her personal beliefs were placed in the mouth of the Misfit.

The resurrection of Jesus Christ changes everything.

We might say, to use an odd metaphor, that Christ's resurrection has many tentacles. That is, it touches countless aspects of our lives, both present and future, thereby magnifying its importance.

These areas are worthy of serious thought.

## The Resurrection and Salvation

What does the resurrection of Jesus have to do with our salvation?

In a word, everything.

Let's prove it.

## Belief: The Resurrection Personalized

It goes without saying that we must believe in the truth of the resurrection, which one scholar described as "the best-attested fact in human history."[9]

Our salvation, however, does not come from subscribing dispassionately to a truth claim.

We must believe that the resurrection was *for us*.

Tim Keller distilled the essence of Christianity in delivering another sermon on the theme:

> The essence of Christianity is personal pronouns. If you are here this morning saying, "The Son of God was born, he died, he was raised, he ascended, and he's coming again," that doesn't make you a Christian. But if you say, "The Son of God was born *for me*, he died *for me*, he was raised *for me*, he was ascended to the right hand of the Father *for me*, and

---

9 Thomas Arnold, quoted in Wayne Jackson (2005), *The Acts of the Apostles: From Jerusalem to Rome*, p. 218.

he's going to come again *for me*," that's the essence of Christianity.

Paul says it in Romans 4:25. He says Jesus Christ was raised *for* our justification. You're not a Christian and you don't understand Christianity if you just understand Jesus was raised. You have to understand he was raised *for* us. Paul says, "for our salvation."[10]

This surely is what Paul had in mind when he wrote:

If you confess with your mouth that Jesus is Lord and believe in your heart that God raised him from the dead, you will be saved. (Romans 10:9)

We must internalize the resurrection. We must personalize it.

It is an "in-your-heart" belief.

## Baptism: The Resurrection Reenacted

Just as salvation does not stem from a cold, hard, fact, it also does not issue merely from passive mental assent.

In 1 Corinthians 15:3-4, Paul reminded his readers of the heart of the gospel.

For I delivered to you as of first importance what I also received: that Christ died for our sins in accordance with the Scriptures, that he was buried,

---

[10] Tim Keller (1991). "I Am the Resurrection and the Life." Sermon delivered at Redeemer Presbyterian Church, March 31, 1991.

that he was raised on the third day in accordance with
the Scriptures....

Central to the saving message is the death, burial, and
resurrection of Jesus.

In the first few verses of Romans 6, the same apostle said
that in coming to Christ, we imitate a replica (v. 17) of this
teaching.

> What shall we say then? Are we to continue in sin
> that grace may abound? By no means! How can we
> who died to sin still live in it? Do you not know that
> all of us who have been baptized into Christ Jesus
> were baptized into his death? We were buried
> therefore with him by baptism into death, in order
> that, just as Christ was raised from the dead by the
> glory of the Father, we too might walk in newness of
> life.

Notice the close connection between 1 Corinthians 15 and
Romans 6.

Jesus died (1 Corinthians 15:3).

Jesus was buried (1 Corinthians 15:4).

Jesus rose again (1 Corinthians 15:4).

We die...to sin (Romans 6:2).

We are buried...in baptism (Romans 6:4).

We are raised...to walk in newness of life (Romans 6:4).

As Peter related in 1 Peter 3:21:

Baptism, which corresponds to this, now saves you, not as a removal of dirt from the body but as an appeal to God for a good conscience, through the resurrection of Jesus Christ…

Notice carefully:

Baptism…now saves you…through the resurrection of Jesus Christ.

We sometimes fail to make the proper emphasis here.

Apart from the resurrection of Christ, baptism would have no meaning. It is the resurrection which gives baptism its significance, not vice versa. At the same time, it must be admitted that many in the modern religious world have not appreciated the multi-layered beauty of this sacred ordinance.

May God help us all to properly revere the resurrection of the Son of God—and to better understand baptism, which pictures it.

## Future Judgment: The Resurrection's Guarantee

In his speech before the skeptical Athenians, Paul warned that God demands repentance from everyone (Acts 17:30).

The prime motivation for such a life-altering decision, Paul affirmed, is God's coming judgment.

Because he has fixed a day on which he will judge the world in righteousness by a man whom he has appointed; and of this he has given assurance to all by raising him from the dead (Acts 17:31).

The idea of divine judgment is little more than a joke to some. It was to more than a few of the Athenians, who mocked at the mention of the resurrection.

Others were not as dismissive. "We will hear you again about this," they said (Acts 17:32).

But the question is eminently practical.

How can we be sure that one day we will stand before the God of the universe to give an account for how we have lived?

Did you see what Paul said?

"He has given assurance to all by raising him from the dead."

Someone asks, "Do you *really* believe that you will stand before God one day?"

Yes, I do.

And you will stand before him, as well.

We can be certain of that.

It's a sobering thought.

And it's all because Jesus came back from the dead.

## "No Ordinary People"

I told you earlier in this chapter that Timothy Keller's hero was C.S. Lewis.

I may not have said it in those exact words, but that was the idea.

Keller is not the only person to admire C.S. Lewis, you know.

In 1941, Lewis delivered a sermon at the Church of St. Mary the Virgin in Oxford, England. The sermon was transcribed and later included with a collection of other Lewis material and published in book form as *The Weight of Glory*. If you've never read that particular address, you should stop and read it now.

Go ahead. Google it. It's a free read.

It's okay. I'll be here when you get back.


[Second Intermission]


So, what did you think about it?

I told you it was good.

Here's my favorite part.

One of them, at least.

> The dullest and most uninteresting person you talk to may one day be a creature which, if you saw it now, you would be strongly tempted to worship, or else a

horror and a corruption such as you meet, if at all, only in a nightmare.[11]

Then there's this. It's really my favorite.

"There are no *ordinary* people. You have never talked to a mere mortal."

Why are there no ordinary people?

Because of Jesus.

Because he rose from the dead.

Because of Jesus…

- We will live forever (1 Thessalonians 4:17),
- in a glorified body (Philippians 3:21),
- with the King of kings and Lord of lords (Revelation 17:14),
- in the unadulterated presence of God the Father (Revelation 21:3),
- in the new heavens and new earth (Revelation 21:1),
- with the redeemed of all the ages (Revelation 7:9),
- including the kings of the earth (Revelation 21:24),
- and, what is sweet to our human hearts, with our loved ones who have gone before (2 Samuel 12:23).

Doesn't that make you want to give your heart to Jesus?

Doesn't that make you want to live for him, in the here and now?

---

[11] C.S. Lewis (1949), *The Weight of Glory*, p. 45.

It should.

**Say What You Mean to Say**

Allow me to make one last C.S. Lewis reference…at least in this chapter. Even if it's not exactly flattering to his readers, myself among them.

Here it is:

Lewis believed that writing is like herding cattle.

I love that analogy, even if it makes a bovine out of me.

His point was this: If there is a divergent path your readers can take, they will take it.

So write clearly.

Keep your readers on the right path.

I have wanted to be so clear in what I have written thus far—the serious stuff, at least—so that the preciousness of Christ's resurrection will be etched onto your heart.

At one point, I had thought about saying something like this.

"If Christianity were an onion, and you peeled back all the layers, one at a time, at the center would be the resurrection of Jesus."

But I felt like that sentence teetered on the brink of something.

And what it was, was not good.[12]

So instead I'll say this.

The resurrection of Christ is not just a fact to be believed.

Or a creed to be defended.

Though, as we have seen, it is both.

The resurrection is what gives life meaning.

Without it, nothing else would matter.

And the beauty of that is…the simplicity of that is…it doesn't change.

You can claim it when you are elated.

You can cling to it when you're absolutely broken.

Because it won't change. It can't change.

But it changes us.

For time…

…and for eternity.

---

[12] In the first book I ever penned, over fifteen years ago, there was a chapter in which I imagined going back in time to the first century, in order to compare the early church with the church of today. This sentence *almost* made it into the book: "As the elders escort you back to the time machine…" But I scrubbed it. It would have been, quite possibly, the worst sentence published in the history of Western literature.

# Chapter 4

# A Better Resurrection

In the home where I grew up, there is a painting.

For Christmas in 1958, just their second as a married couple, my parents were given a gift any right-thinking newlywed couple would covet.

A pressure cooker.

Inexplicably, for reasons known only to them, they chose to return this finest of culinary implements. In its place they selected an oil painting,[1] which took up long-term residence with my family.[2]

It was lost, once, well before I was born. When my Navy family moved from Great Lakes, Illinois, to Tiverton, Rhode Island, in 1967, the painting was misplaced in transit. Fortunately, it was recovered—though the details of its rescue are sketchy at best. Suffice it to say that by the time I arrived on the scene in 1978, the painting (and my family) had relocated to Alabama.

The landscape portrays a peaceful autumnal scene, with a curving country path snaking through a forest clearing, narrowing as it goes. In the distance, the sun is shining, its

---

[1] Bennett-Knight furniture store in Piedmont, Alabama. I love any place that sells oil paintings and pressure cookers.
[2] It's still hanging there now, as of May 2020. They don't make oil paintings like this anymore, kids.

rays piercing evenly through several small openings in the clouds.

We used to play pretend with this painting, when I was a boy.

My dad said that a possum lurked under a rock in it.

My older brother, Steve, was convinced that he went fishing in the painting, in a pond just out of sight, not far around the bend.[3]

My sister, Cheryl, didn't say much about the painting.

She just thought we were crazy, I suppose.

Or maybe her adventures were her own.

Today, far removed from childhood, it's difficult to describe the feelings evoked by this painting. No single sentiment perfectly captures the mood. I know that happiness is one element, as is the nostalgia felt in recalling simpler times. But there also is a touch of sadness: a sense that we are, and must remain, short of ultimate bliss in this life.

**"Joy"**

Transcendence is an elusive mistress.

If you aim for it, you are almost certain to miss.

---

[3] He also convinced me in the early 1980s that he was a member of the rock group, Journey. When I expressed some degree of skepticism, he proceeded to sing their songs. He knew the lyrics! My brother was in Journey!

It's not easy to define, much less to explain.

The Germans call it *Sehnsucht*.

C.S. Lewis, mercifully, did not call it that.

But he talked about it.

A lot.

In fact, I would argue that regardless of his theme—from the *Chronicles of Narnia* to *Mere Christianity*, and all points in between—he wrote of little else. The idea permeates every square inch of his writing.

He called it "Joy"—capital J—though he didn't mean happiness, or even pleasure, exactly. "Joy is distinct not only from pleasure in general," he insisted, "but even from aesthetic pleasure. It must have the stab, the pang, the inconsolable longing."[4] There is a "bitterness," he wrote elsewhere, "which mixes with the sweetness."[5]

Sometimes Lewis could be rather technical when pontificating on the subject.

"The human soul was made to enjoy some object that is never fully given—nay, cannot even be imagined as given—in our present mode of subjective and spatio-temporal experience."[6]

On other occasions, his words approached the sublime.

---

[4] C.S. Lewis, *Surprised by Joy* (1955), p. 72.
[5] C.S. Lewis, *The Weight of Glory* (1949), p. 40.
[6] C.S. Lewis, *The Pilgrim's Regress* (2014), p. 204-205.

> [Joy is] that unnamable something, desire for which pierces us like a rapier at the smell of a bonfire, the sound of wild ducks flying overhead, the title of *The Well at the World's End*, the opening lines of *Kubla Khan*, the morning cobwebs in late summer, or the noise of falling waves....[7]

My dear friend and editor,[8] Drew Kizer, has encountered Joy in the works of Russian filmmaker Andrei Tarkovsky. Lewis found it in varied places, though he could never command it to appear. He called it "the secret signature of each soul."[9]

I feel certain that the ancient king, Solomon, was acquainted with Joy.

Like C.S. Lewis, he wrote of it, too.

Solomon even tells us the source of the wistful emotion.

"He has put eternity into man's heart," was his explanation (Ecclesiastes 3:11).

What is the source of this "mysterious something we are all after"?[10]

God himself, according to the wise king.

---

[7] Ibid., p. 204.

[8] He is not to be blamed for any of my footnotes.

[9] C.S. Lewis, *The Problem of Pain* (1978), p. 134.

[10] C.S. Lewis, *Mere Christianity* (2001), pp. 135-136.

Every so often, we get a glimpse—a whisper on the breeze—not of how things are, but of how things should be.

How they could be.

How they will be, one day.

## My Sister, the Educator

Which brings me to my sister.

She's the reason I'm writing this.

One of the reasons, at least.

She's also why, incidentally, I refer to myself as a teacher, as opposed to an educator.

The distinction is an arbitrary one, I suppose, but in my mind it goes like this: a teacher instructs students, while an educator instructs other teachers.

However you decide to parse it, my sister was an educator in the truest sense of the word.

She taught kindergarten for many years before becoming a media specialist and a reading coach. She could check out your books and teach you how to read them, all in one stop.

She later served in a central office position, being responsible for writing and implementing continuous improvement plans—CIPs, for those of you in the know.

In 1991, she was named Anniston (AL) City Schools Elementary Teacher of the Year. She later was the first teacher in her school system to become National Board Certified. I am proud of what she accomplished, if you can't tell.

She was poised to begin work on her doctoral dissertation when, in December 2012, she was diagnosed unexpectedly with Stage 4 colon cancer.

She was 54 years old.

Once, when researching this awful disease on the internet, she came across something that made her laugh, if only to keep from crying.

"Do you know what the recommendation is for a Stage 4 colon cancer patient?" she asked me.

"What?"

"Donate your body to science."

At least she kept her sense of humor, even if it was gallows humor.

I remember the night she told me about her diagnosis.

"Of course I want to live," she said.

"But if I don't, I think about who'll be waiting for me on the other side."

She was thinking, I know, about her daddy.

She confessed Christ as Lord and was baptized on April 30, 2013.

She died eleven days later.

**A Better Resurrection**

"What does any of this have to do," someone asks, "with the resurrection of the dead?"

Well, everything, my friend.

Just everything.

A common Protestant idea seems to be—and some of our Catholic friends may imbibe it as well, for all I know— that heaven is a wispy, ethereal place in a netherworld, somehow less "real" and less vibrant than our current sphere of existence.

And when you die, if you've been good enough, eventually you'll get to go there. It won't erase the indignities of this present life, but at least you won't have to suffer them anymore. This view pictures heaven almost like a spiritual retirement community, a consolation prize, for those who've put their years in, so to speak.

But it is *not* the biblical idea of heaven.

For the believer, the world to come is part of what the Hebrews writer described as "a better resurrection" (Hebrews 11:35, KJV/ASV).

Jesus, as you know, was not the first person in the Bible to return to life from the dead. There were even contemporaries of Christ who came back from the grave—Lazarus, for instance. But these and other examples we could provide—the daughter of Jairus, the widow of Nain's son—are better understood as "resuscitations" than as "resurrections."

Why?

Because, as Tim Keller noted,

> Even though the person came back to life, they're still subject to suffering, they're still subject to disease, they're still subject to death. In other words, the terrible day has just been put off. Escape from suffering is only ever temporary; escape from death is only ever temporary.[11]

Keller makes an excellent point.

Yes, these individuals came back to life.

But the "terrible day" was just delayed.

Death came calling again for every single person that Jesus or the apostles raised.

But Jesus was resurrected, never to die again (Romans 6:9).

And, because of him, death one day will be reversed.

It will be defeated.

---

[11] Tim Keller (2005). Sermon: "A Better Resurrection." Redeemer Presbyterian Church, March 27, 2005.

Not just defeated—it will be absolutely destroyed (1 Corinthians 15:26).

"Did you hear about death? It has passed away," one day we'll boast (Revelation 21:4).

The irony will be delicious.

**Leaves that Heal**

In John's vision of a new heaven and a new earth (Revelation 21:1), the tree of life is pictured once again "in the paradise of God" (Revelation 22:2). Once it blossomed in the midst of the original Garden paradise (Genesis 2:9), and now it blooms forevermore.

Fruit is plentiful on this tree, and nothing is forbidden.

But its leaves are what capture our attention.

John makes us privy to their secret:

"The leaves of the tree are for the healing of the nations" (Revelation 22:2).

Do you see that?

Heaven will not merely compensate for our earthly sufferings. For the lies that others slandered us with. For cruel betrayals. For whatever slings and arrows this life had thrown our way.

No, heaven will be the great reversal of all wrongs.

God himself has promised us.

"Behold, I am making all things new" (Revelation 21:5).

As Tim Keller relates, Jesus is saying, in essence: "Embrace me…and everything that goes wrong in your life, every sorrow, I eventually will turn to gold." Keller continues: "Through the resurrection of Jesus Christ, every one of your sorrows will eventually make your eventual glory greater, your eventual joy greater. I don't know how, but it will, and that's the ultimate defeat of evil."[12]

**The Road That Will Take Us Home**

I never forgot about the painting in my boyhood home.

The road, the leaves, the sun.

We all were together there, once.

In June 2003, just days after we laid my father to rest, I went to the theater with my wife to see the newly released film, *Gods and Generals*.

It was a Civil War epic, which is a genre I love, but it was produced by Ted Turner.

I wasn't expecting much.

I certainly wasn't prepared for the opening credits.

Onto the wide screen burst beautiful images of state flags, tattered vestiges of a bygone era, accompanied by the sound of a breeze, as the banners gently unfurled.

---

[12] *Ibid.*

Into the dark of the quiet theatre came the mournful voice
of Mary Fahl.[13]

As I listened, tears welled in my eyes, just as they had on
that afternoon in May, when I was with my dad, in the
rose garden.

*They say there's a place,*

*Where dreams have all gone*

*They never said where,*

*But I think I know*

*It's miles through the night,*

*Just over the dawn*

*On the road that will take me home*

---

[13] If you're interested, go to YouTube and search for "Gods and Generals Opening
Titles with Mary Fahl's 'Going Home.'" Watch it on a full screen. In a quiet and
preferably dark room. If transcendent moments can be shared—if Joy can be
shared—and I don't know that it can—then I am sharing mine with you.

# Recommended Reading on the Resurrection

I'm going to make a promise to you just here. I think it's a pretty unique one, if I do say so myself.

I'm only going to recommend books that I've read the majority of. In my opinion, over half the books that end up on similar lists are the result of a quick Google search. As if to say, "Yeah, that's a book on this subject. Let's include it."

That's why I can't recommend (I'm so sorry, I really don't mean to pick on him) N. T. Wright's, *The Resurrection of the Son of God*. By now, you know it's available. If you decide to read it—all of it, now, not just cherry-picking—please do let me know.[1]

## Books by Gary Habermas

All three of these are debates Habermas held with Antony Flew. I prefer these books to Habermas' stand-alone works. I think it's because there's lively discussion to keep you engaged.

- *Did Jesus Rise From The Dead? The Resurrection Debate* (1987)
- *Resurrected? An Atheist and Theist Dialogue* (2005)—my favorite of the three

---

[1] Email should be directed to bcrenfroe@dekalbk12.org. That's my school address. Be sure to put "Not an Angry Parent" in the subject line, so I'll know not to delete it.

- *Did the Resurrection Happen? A Conversation with Gary Habermas and Antony Flew* (2009)

## Books by Tim Keller

To my knowledge, Keller hasn't written a single volume devoted exclusively to the resurrection. He has, however, addressed the subject in other works. My favorite is:

- *The Reason for God: Belief in an Age of Skepticism* (2009)

The best two chapters in this book, in my judgment, are chapters 12 and 13. Chapter 12 is "The (True) Story of the Cross" and Chapter 13 is "The Reality of the Resurrection." If you read nothing else in this book, you'll want to read these. Keller is wonderful, even if he would differ with me on a few things.

## Two Other Books I Think You Might Like

Rather than continuing to say, "Books by…" when there's only one book, I want to mention these two, ranked in the order in which I like them.

- *Truth Matters: Confident Faith in a Confusing World* (2014)

This book—the entire book[2]—is one that I highly recommend for high school and college-aged kids. The authors tackle a variety of subjects that skeptical professors often twist in seeking to overthrow the faith of impressionable students. The existence of God, the

---

[2] Really, it's more like a handbook, which I also like.

problem of evil, and the inspiration of the Bible are all addressed. My favorite chapter is the last one, chapter 7: "A Likely Story" (How Do We Know Jesus Rose From the Dead?). In fact, this may be my single favorite volume on apologetics. It's relatively short (a must), accessible, and has a green cover. I don't know why, but I think it looks cool. Really, you should have purchased *Truth Matters* rather than my book.[3]

- *I Don't Have Enough Faith to be an Atheist* (2004)

This excellent volume is by Norman Geisler and Frank Turek. I very much like Frank Turek's book *Stealing From God: Why Atheists Need God to Make Their Case* (2015), so I'm going to blame Mr. Geisler[4] for the minor qualms I have with this volume, which may be distilled to two: (1) It's rather long (which may not bother you at all) and (2) Though it may seem picky, I believe this book uses the word "faith" in an incorrect fashion, and to the point of annoyance.

In other words, the authors suggest that there are so many more things you'd have to blindly accept to be an atheist, as opposed to a theist, that it makes more sense to be a theist. That's true. But the way they state this—and they do it repeatedly—is, "We don't have enough faith to believe that!" (in other words, to accept whatever outlandish claim of atheism they are criticizing). But faith, in the biblical sense, is a good thing. It is something we need to cultivate and increase. It is based on evidence, not

---

[3] No worries, as I'm guessing I gave you this copy. Or else you paid $5 for it on Amazon. So it's not like I'm getting rich.
[4] I kid, I kid.

a blind leap in the dark. So the (surely unintended) implication of their pet statement is, "If we just had more faith, we'd become atheists." Did no editor call this to their attention during the proofing process?

But these are minor complaints. Even if I harped on them too long. The chapter on the resurrection— "Did Jesus Really Rise from the Dead?" —is worth the price of the entire book. It helped me tremendously.

# Afterword
# Drew Kizer

Diabetes is very common and manageable in most cases, but a few of its unfortunate victims lose circulation in their extremities to the point that amputation becomes necessary. I had a friend who fell into this category of diabetics with the worst symptoms. Diabetes took him, literally, one piece at a time. First it was a few toes, then his hand, then one of his legs.

Even after the first few surgeries, he continued to teach Bible class. He remained cheerful and encouraged others who dealt with physical disabilities by demonstrating that it was possible to keep a good attitude and remain productive despite the ravages of a crippling disease.

In many ways, he was an inspiration. But if I might be candid, one thing he repeatedly said while teaching Bible class made me squirm in my pew. "People ask me," he said, "how do you deal with the loss of your hand? I tell them, *It's just dirt.* Our bodies are just dirt! And when we die, our souls will leave these bodies to dwell eternally with God."

He had verses of Scripture to back him up. For example, Ecclesiastes 12:7 says, "… the dust returns to the earth as it was, and the spirit returns to God who gave it." Also, James defines physical death in terms of separation in James 2:26: "For as the body apart from the spirit is dead, so also faith apart from works is dead." The Bible teaches that at death the body returns to the earth, while the soul goes to be with God.

But does that mean our bodies are just dirt? Is that all they are to us? Not according to Scripture. You see, the separation of the body from the spirit at death is only half of the story. When Christ returns, our spirits will experience a reunion with our bodies. And that applies to every person, whether he is righteous or wicked. Jesus said, "Do not marvel at this, for an hour is coming when all who are in the tombs will hear his voice and come out, those who have done good to the resurrection of life, and those who have done evil to the resurrection of judgment" (John 5:28-29). Every life anticipates resurrection, but for the righteous, resurrection means a new, glorified body. Paul preached this hope, promising that when Jesus returns, he "will transform our lowly body to be like his glorious body, by the power that enables him even to subject all things to himself" (Philippians 3:21).

If this is where history is headed—to the return of Christ and the resurrection of all our bodies—then in terms of punctuation, physical death is only a comma, not a period. God will redeem not only our souls but also our bodies (Romans 8:23). And if that is true, our bodies matter.

Something within us knows this to be true, even if we deny it with bad theology. Why else do we use anti-aging cream, and why is cosmetic surgery a multibillion-dollar industry?[1] Why do we shriek at horror movies in which

---

[1] $16 billion, to be exact. "More than $16 Billion Spent on Cosmetic Plastic Surgery," *American Society of Plastic Surgeons* (April 12, 2017), www.plasticsurgery.org/news/press-releases/more-than-16-billion-spent-on-cosmetic-plastic-surgery.

bodies are harmed in gruesome ways? Why is history filled with stories of cruel conquerors mutilating the bodies of vanquished kings?[2] Why did Moses decree that the Israelites should not leave the bodies of the condemned hanging all night from a tree because "a hanged man is cursed by God"? (Deuteronomy 21:23). Why do we regard suicide, an act committed against the body but powerless against the soul, as something so terrible? Why do we instinctively seek to preserve our lives and take care of our bodies? (cf. Ephesians 5:29). Why do we embalm the bodies of our loved ones after they die and have funerals? Why do we wash them and dress them and lay them in beautiful caskets? Why do we bury them in beautiful cemeteries instead of throwing them into the garbage dump? Why do we hear legends about the preservation of the bodies of saints?[3] Why do doctors take the Hippocratic oath to "do no harm"? Why did Ponce de Leon look for the fountain of youth?

I will tell you why. Because our bodies are not just "dirt." They may die, but they will rise. *Bodies matter.* And God raised his Son from the dead to prove this (1 Corinthians 15:20; Colossians 1:18).

Since the resurrection gives us a proper estimation of the value of our bodies, we should spend some time contemplating the purpose for these vessels of the soul,

---

[2] The Philistines did this to King Saul (1 Samuel 31:9).

[3] "Incorruptibility" is a Roman Catholic and Eastern Orthodox superstition that the bodies of some saints do not undergo the normal process of decomposition as a sign of their holiness. Similarly, it is said that the body of Polycarp gave off a sweet aroma, like frankincense, when it was burned at the stake. Fyodor Dostoevsky alludes to these legends in *The Brothers Karamazov* when Alyosha grieves over the decomposition of his beloved mentor, Zosima.

now jars of clay (2 Corinthians 4:7)—but, one day, something more glorious.

One thing is for sure: bodies are not made for a sedentary lifestyle. One of the most common workplace injuries is carpal tunnel syndrome. According to the Mayo Clinic, the health risks of sitting still for more than eight hours a day include obesity, high blood pressure, high blood sugar, abnormal cholesterol levels, cardiovascular disease, and cancer.[4] Our bodies are not designed for sitting. They were made to be active—to work, run, play, serve, and stay active.

Where, then, do we get the idea that heaven, a habitation for resurrected bodies, will be an airy, nebulous retirement home cushioned with puffy white clouds, where there is little to do but take naps and occasionally play the harp? While I would like to believe this view of heaven has come into my mind from cartoons about cats meeting their untimely demise at the hands of clever mice, I know that I have heard it described in conversations, books, and even Bible classes and sermons. When we hear the word "heaven," the first thought in many of our minds is not a world buzzing with activity but one inhabited by careful apparitions tiptoeing alone in misty, halcyon fields, doing nothing.

If this inert view of heaven has any biblical basis, I suppose it comes from those passages that speak of our eternal dwelling place in terms of "rest." Pointing to heaven as the reality foreshadowed by the Sabbath, the

---

[4] Edward R. Laskowski, "What are the risks of sitting too much?" *Mayo Clinic*, www.mayoclinic.org/healthy-lifestyle/adult-health/expert-answers/sitting/faq-20058005.

writer of Hebrews assures us that "there remains a Sabbath rest for the people of God" (Hebrews 4:9). In the book of Revelation, John heard a voice from heaven commanding him to write, "Blessed are the dead who die in the Lord from now on…that they may rest from their labors, for their deeds follow them!" (Revelation 14:13). Heaven will be a place of rest, but are we supposed to equate rest with leisure? That is certainly one definition of rest, but is that the only way to look at it?

The Bible speaks of rest in terms of changed activity rather than simple leisure. Numerous examples can be listed. God did not cease all activity when he "rested" on the seventh day (Genesis 2:2; cf. John 5:17). Also, the Israelites did not stop all activity when they entered the rest of the Promised Land. Their lives in Canaan involved hard work. They did escape from oppressive toil, insecurity, homelessness, uncertainty, struggle, and fear. Their inheritance was to be an active, yet peaceful and prosperous existence, filled with the manifold blessings of God. Furthermore, the Sabbath day was not the cessation of all activity. On the seventh day of the week, the Israelites cared for themselves and their families, interacted with friends and relatives, worshiped God, ate together, and did many other activities. Sabbath-work was different than the activity on the other six days of the week, but it was still activity.

Just so, heaven will be a place of rest, but it will be buzzing with activity. We are not given specifics, but the pictures of heaven John saw in the book of Revelation support the idea of heaven as a place where the saints will be eternally employed. Revelation 7:15-17 reads,

Therefore they are before the throne of God, and serve him day and night in his temple; and he who sits on the throne will shelter them with his presence. They shall hunger no more, neither thirst anymore; the sun shall not strike them, nor any scorching heat. For the Lamb in the midst of the throne will be their shepherd, and he will guide them to springs of living water, and God will wipe away every tear from their eyes.

Revelation 22:3 says, "No longer will there be anything accursed, but the throne of God and of the Lamb will be in it, and his servants will worship him." There will be work, but unlike our work on earth, it will not be accompanied by toil, frustration, disappointment, and fatigue. Heaven will restore the activity that humanity has not seen since the Fall, when the sweat began to fall from Adam's brow and thorns and thistles sprouted from God's once-fertile ground (Genesis 3:17-19).

The promise of a busy heaven, it seems to me, is good news. Voltaire said, "Rest is a good thing, but boredom is its brother." One or two days with nothing to do might be pleasurable; but imagine an eternity of dormancy. It sounds more like hibernation than bliss.

The specifics of our heavenly work, as I said, have not been given. We do not need to know all the details. God gave us plenty to do in this world, and he is perfectly capable of keeping us busy in the next. We do know this: whatever our work will be, it will be pure, joyful, and centered upon God.

One day, we will enjoy unburdened, joyful service in heaven. What are we to do in the meantime? Listen to Peter:

> Since all these things are thus to be dissolved, what sort of people ought you to be in lives of holiness and godliness, waiting for and hastening the coming of the day of God, because of which the heavens will be set on fire and dissolved, and the heavenly bodies will melt as they burn! But according to his promise we are waiting for new heavens and a new earth in which righteousness dwells. (2 Peter 3:11-13)

Because one day we will be engaged in righteous activity in heaven, we should start living out that existence now, to the best of our ability, by leading lives of "holiness and godliness." John says essentially the same thing in 1 John 3:2-3:

> Beloved, we are God's children now, and what we will be has not yet appeared; but we know that when he appears we shall be like him, because we shall see him as he is. And everyone who thus hopes in him purifies himself as he is pure.

Darrell Bock described this anticipation of heaven as "pulling the future into the present and previewing the future in the present."[5]

In the excellent volume you just read, Brandon challenges us to live out the resurrection in this life. If Jesus really rose from the dead, and we believe that his resurrection is

---

[5] Unpublished document cited in Ralph Gilmore, "The Magnificence of the Word 'Kingdom,'" *Kingdom* (1:1).

a sign that we, too, will rise from the dead, our lives should be changed by this belief. This is the "living hope" Peter describes in 1 Peter 1:3. As people who believe in heaven, we have a hope that matters, one that forecasts the glory of our hopeful expectations. We live differently from unbelievers in this life, not just because God told us to, but because after his Son died on the cross for our sins, he brought him back to life in a glorious body. That makes all the difference.